Helen Keller
Leader Without Sight or Sound

Darren J. Butler

Seacoast Publishing
Birmingham, Alabama

Helen Keller: Leader Without Sight or Sound

Published by Seacoast Publishing, Inc.
1149 Mountain Oaks Drive
Birmingham, Alabama 35226

Copyright © 2012 Darren J. Butler

All rights reserved.
Reviewers and writers of magazine and newspaper articles are free to quote passages of this book as needed for their work. Otherwise, no part of this book may be reproduced or transmitted in any form or by any means, electronic or mechanical, including photocopying, recording or by any information storage and retrieval system, without the written permission of the publisher.

Library of Congress Control Number: 2012930105

Cover art by Thomas B. Moore

ISBN 978-1-59421-083-9

To obtain copies of this book, please write or call:
Seacoast Publishing, Inc.
Post Office Box 26492
Birmingham, Alabama 35260
(205) 979-2909

Darren J. Butler

Contents

"Her Name is Helen Adams Keller" 16

Spring, 1886 24

Meeting Dr. Bell 27

The Endless Train Ride To Tuscumbia 40

Student Meets Teacher 56

The Spoiled Child 63

The Fight 72

The Little House 79

Water 89

Helen Keller, A True Citizen Of The World 99

Timeline 104

About The Author 108

Helen Keller: Leader Without Sight or Sound
About The Series

Alabama Roots is a book series designed to provide reading pleasure for young people, to allow readers to better know the men and women who shaped the State of Alabama, and to fill a much-needed void of quality regional non-fiction for students in middle grades.

For years, teachers and librarians have searched for quality biographies about famous people from Alabama. This series is a response to that search. The series will cover a span of time from pre-statehood through the modern day.

The goal of *Alabama Roots* is to provide biographies that are historically accurate and as interesting as the characters whose lives they explore.

The *Alabama Roots* mark assures readers and educators of consistent quality in research, composition, and presentation.

It is a joint publishing project of Seacoast Publishing, Inc., and Will Publishing, Inc., both located in Birmingham, Alabama.

Editor's Note: The Alabama Roots Biography Series handles quotations in two ways.

Quotes that can be found in the historical record are used inside quotation marks.

Occasionally, authors flesh out a scene from the historical record by creating dialogue so that the event

Darren J. Butler

is told in first person. In those cases when the actual words are not on the historical record, the dialogue is in italic type and not inside quotation marks.

That is the case with this biography of Helen Keller. The difference is that there is a great deal more dialogue in italics than in any other biography in the Alabama Roots series.

Our author, Darren J. Butler, is director of The Miracle Worker play at Ivy Green, which dramatizes the story of Helen Keller and her teacher Annie Sullivan. Mr. Butler has studied Miss Keller's life extensively and as director of the play, wanted to tell this story with greater use of the dialogue style.

Each scene in this book is a part of the historical record and Mr. Butler has been meticulous in his research.

In those instances where dialogue is in quotation marks, the actual words were located in the historical record of Miss Keller's life.

In those instances were Mr. Butler chose to use dialogue to tell the story, but the actual works are not on the historical record, the dialogue is in italic type.

Dedication

I would like to dedicate this book to the following...

To my dear friend and mentor WILLIAM GIBSON.

SUE PILKILTON for a lifetime of love and dedication to the Helen Keller Birthplace.

THE BOARD MEMBERS OF THE HELEN KELLER BIRTHPLACE who continue to honor Helen Keller.

KELLER JOHNSON-THOMPSON who continues the work of her great aunt.

THE CAST OF "THE MIRACLE WORKER" PAST AND PRESENT for telling Helen and Annie's story.
&
MY WIFE, FREDA, who continues to inspire and support me every day to do what I love to do.

Darren J. Butler

Writing This Book

When I do author visits at schools or go into a classroom as a writing specialist, one of the common questions is, "How long does it take to write a book?" Each time, I laugh. This leads to the next question, "Mr. Butler...what's so funny?"

My answer is "Helen Keller - a Biography." I have to explain that my deadline for the book passed a long time ago, and my publisher has been incredibly patient. Normally, I can write a book in as little as three months, but "Helen Keller" was a different story all together. To understand this, you will have to indulge me in a little personal history...

In 1999, I took over the job of directing *The Miracle Worker* at Ivy Green, Helen Keller's Birthplace. The play started in 1961 as an outdoor drama on the grounds where Helen was born, played, and the miracle occurred. The play was named the Official Outdoor Drama for the State of Alabama and has remained one of the top tourist attractions for the state.

Helen Keller: Leader Without Sight or Sound

I had attended the play with my students for a number of years. In 1993, I produced the play in my hometown of Decatur and brought the Ivy Green cast over for the production. Thus began my relationship with Ivy Green and the play's director at the time, David Hope. The following summer, I stage managed the play for Mr. Hope and was thrilled to be a part of the production. When Mr. Hope retired in 1998, I applied for the position and was ecstatic to get the job. I am now in my 13th year as the Resident Director of *The Miracle Worker* at Helen Keller's Birthplace. We celebrated the 50th anniversary of the play in the summer of 2011.

However, this became a problem in writing this book. I know the script for *The Miracle Worker* backwards and forwards. I can quote it word for word. I had the privilege of knowing William Gibson, who wrote the play, and corresponded with him at his home in Stockbridge, Massachusetts for years before his death. The issue lies in the fact that the play and the actual story are different. For dramatic purposes, Mr. Gibson had to make the story of Helen's young life fit into the dramatic structure of a play. To do that, many things had to change.

For starters, Captain Keller's sons—James and Simpson—from his first marriage were combined into one character, James. Although Kate Keller is depicted quite accurately, Captain Keller is more forceful and commanding than the actual man.

The dialogue between the characters in the play was made up to move the story along. That dialogue runs through my head constantly! When I was writing this book, I had to turn off that stream of words so I wouldn't put them in this book. I had to think like Annie, the Captain, Kate and Ev in order to imagine what they would say in the different situations.

In the play, the scenes between Annie and Helen are historically accurate, but the scenes that fall in between those moments are only loosely based on fact. A huge difference lies in the final scene where Helen's miracle takes place. The play and movie portray a fight at the dinner table following Helen's two-week stay in the Little House. Helen tries to go back to her old ways and spills the water pitcher. Annie drags her out of the house to refill the pitcher. In reality, this never happened. It makes great drama for the stage and the screen, but Helen's miracle at the pump happened just the way I describe it in this book. How do I know? I used *The Story of My Life* by Helen Keller, *Anne Sullivan Macy* by Nella Braddy Henney, and copies of typed pages by Annie Sullivan that describe the events that happened.

Helen Keller: Leader Without Sight or Sound

Writing this book has definitely been a journey! I've had the opportunity to meet and work with some amazing people along the way. For starters, William Gibson was a major influence in my writing and my love of "two of the most famous women in American history" as he referred to them. Bill, as he liked to be called, faithfully wrote me letters and e-mails. He encouraged me as a writer and as a director. On one occasion I had the privilege of visiting him at his home in Stockbridge, Massachusetts. On this particular visit, Arthur Penn was in attendance! Mr. Penn directed the original Broadway play and the motion picture that won many Oscars. Having the two of them to consult with me on our production at Ivy Green was invaluable! In 2003, the play was revived with an intent for a Broadway run, but was cancelled after poor reviews. I was there in Charlotte, North Carolina where the play was being workshopped with Hilary Swank as Annie and Skye McCole Bartusiak as Helen Keller. From my trip to Charlotte, I got to know Skye and her mother Helen, and we continue to work on projects to this day. I'm sure you've heard the old saying, "It's a small world." In the spring of 2010, *The Miracle Worker* was revived on Broadway starring Academy Award Nominee Abigail Breslin as Helen Keller. Skye and Abigail are life-long friends, and this gave me the opportunity

Darren J. Butler

to fly to New York to see the production and meet Abigail. Though their production only ran for a short time, I truly enjoyed seeing another director's insight into my favorite play.

So...if I had a wealth of information at my fingertips, all these amazing people and encounters, "why did it take so long, Mr. Butler?" I've heard this question more times than I can count. I'm sure that my publisher has asked himself this question over and over. The answer is simple - I was frustrated!

This was my first biography. I am accustomed to writing fiction. Since 1990, I've been writing plays and musicals based on fictional characters and situations. In 1998, I published my first novel, *Abbie, Girl Spy - The Case of the Missing Locket*. Three other novels in that series followed the first and I have just published a fantasy novel for children entitled, *Merlin's Curse*. While writing this biography, I've also penned a young adult murder mystery set in 1957 Alabama, several picture books, short stories, and the first half of a general fiction vampire novel called, *Heirloom*. Most recently, I co-wrote a TV series, *Succession*, that is in development with a major cable network. Fiction is easy! I can make it up! I get to decide what happens, what they say, and how it ends! Biographies are incredibly hard because I have to be faithful to the

Helen Keller: Leader Without Sight or Sound

historical events that actually happened. I experienced tremendous stress and pressure while writing this book. As a writing consultant working in schools across the state of Alabama, I imagined students reading this book to learn about the *real* life of Helen Keller. I knew I couldn't make any mistakes. Helen Keller is not only a famous Alabamian—she's one of the most famous citizens of the world that ever lived!

In the end, *Helen Keller* was supposed to be published several years ago. My incredible delay in getting the final manuscript to the publisher has resulted in this biography being one of the last in the series. But you know what? I'm glad. Our state has an incredible history filled with men and women that have played a significant role in shaping our state. However, like I've said more than a few times, Helen Keller was not just a citizen of Alabama, she was a true citizen of the world.

Between March and the end of July, I spend countless hours at Ivy Green preparing *The Miracle Worker* for its six-week run. I have the honor of interacting with thousands of tourists that make a pilgrimage to Helen Keller's birthplace to pay tribute to her life. Many are disabled in some way, but many are not. Her courage and determination to overcome the tremendous obstacles she faced provides every human being with hope.

I hope that you will read more about Helen Keller. Please read *The Story of My Life* as well as the other amazing books about Helen Keller and Annie Sullivan. Watch *The Miracle Worker* with Anne Bancroft and Patty Duke. Take the time to visit Ivy Green in Tuscumbia, Alabama. Ivy Green is not just a tourist attraction. It's a magical place. There is simply no other way to describe it. And, if you happen to visit Ivy Green in the summer, I hope you will attend *The Miracle Worker*! The play is presented on Friday and Saturday nights for six weekends starting in early June and extending through the middle of July. Please visit the website at "http://www.helenkellerbirthplace.org" to find out more about the performance and how to obtain tickets. It will be an experience you'll never forget.

On a final note, I'd like to address the use of dialogue in this book. In a biography, a writer strives to make everything historically accurate. Normally, I would adopt the position of, "if they didn't say it, don't put it in the book." However, there is very little of what they actually said that was written down. I, on the other hand, have had the privilege of living with these people in my head. They are not characters. They are living, breathing people from our past. Next

Helen Keller: Leader Without Sight or Sound

to William Gibson, I would like to think that I know them as well as anyone. Based on the situations, I crafted the dialogue to match the person. Using Annie's written notes on the personalities of the Kellers, I was able to create dialogue that I feel is very accurate to the scenes and situations in this biography. Also, the story of Helen Keller is a story about a little girl who was trapped in a world of silence. Helen was aware that people were talking around her, and she yearned to be able to communicate herself. Therefore, I felt that this biography needed as much dialogue as possible to create the world Helen strived to be a part of.

Darren J. Butler

Helen Adams Keller

Helen Keller: Leader Without Sight or Sound

"Her Name is Helen Adams Keller"

WHAT NAME DO YOU GIVE this child? the minister asked.

Captain Arthur Keller stumbled. In all the excitement surrounding the birth of his daughter, he had forgotten the name they had chosen on the way to the Presbyterian Church! The minister raised his eyebrows, waiting for a response.

Captain Keller looked to his wife and smiled. "Helen Adams Keller."

A bit stunned, Kate Keller beamed. *Thank you, Captain.*

That's quite all right, my dear, he replied. *A lovely name for a lovely child. She has your eyes you know.*

The minister dipped his hand into the basin of water and touched the baby's forehead. "Helen Adams

Keller, I baptize thee in the name of the Father, the Son, and the Holy Ghost. Amen."

Amens echoed throughout the sanctuary from family, friends, and members of the First Presbyterian Church of Tuscumbia, Alabama. Captain Keller and his young wife, Kate, celebrated the baptism of their infant daughter, who had been born a short time before, on June 27th. In 1880, Tuscumbia was a small, sleepy town nestled in the northwestern corner of Alabama.

Kate Keller was a beautiful southern belle from Memphis, Tennessee. She was the second wife to Arthur H. Keller, who had been a captain in the Confederate Army during the Civil War. Everyone, except his older sister Ev, addressed him as "Captain." After their wedding, the couple took up residence at the Keller homestead, which was known as Ivy Green because the house, trees, and fences were covered with beautiful English Ivy.

Captain, Kate said as her husband helped her and the baby descend the carriage. *I thought you wanted to christen her Mildred Campbell Keller?*

Did I? Captain Keller questioned offhandedly.

Kate smiled, trying to hold back her laughter. *I distinctly remember the conversation, Captain. You wanted to name her Mildred Campbell after some ancestor that you seem to hold in high esteem.*

Helen Keller: Leader Without Sight or Sound

Captain Keller held his composure and played along. *Mildred Campbell...Mildred Campbell. Yes, the name does ring a bell.*

Kate cleared her throat. *I, on the other hand, wanted to name her Helen Everett.*

Captain Keller nodded and stroked his chin whiskers. *Well my dear, you got half your wish.*

Arm in arm, the couple strolled down the long, brick walk pushing the stroller toward the small cottage next to the main house. Kate stopped near the porch and kissed her husband on the cheek. *Thank you, Captain.*

"Not at all my dear," he grinned. "Adams is a fine southern name."

My maiden name, least you forget, she teased.

I could never forget, he assured her. *And of course your mother's name is Helen, therefore, Helen Adams along with the Keller surname gives her a unique distinction.*

Kate continued walking towards the steps of the tiny porch. *Mother will be very pleased when I write her.*

I didn't do it for your mother, Captain Keller replied.

Kate turned on her heels and laughed. *You did it because you forgot the name we had chosen!*

Darren J. Butler

I did not! he scoffed.

You did too! Kate fired back.

Unwilling to admit defeat, Captain Keller stood his ground with an eyebrow raised and a slight grin on his face. *It's for the best, my dear.*

Of course it is, Kate agreed as she picked up the baby. *She doesn't look a thing like a Mildred to me. Helen is the perfect name for her.*

As Captain Keller lit his cigar, he added, *We'll name the next one Mildred.*

Whatever you say, Captain.

On Helen's first birthday, she took her first step. Kate had just finished bathing her, when the toddler slipped from her hands and ran towards the flickering shadows of leaves dancing on the floor.

As the summer days faded into fall, the young Helen mastered her first words "tea" and "wah-wah," which of course meant "water." She was a happy, intelligent child with the world at her fingertips. But as the cold winter chill of February approached, a cloud of darkness fell upon Ivy Green.

Aunt Ev quietly knitted in the parlor of the main house. Next door in the Little House, Kate Keller stood horror struck beside Helen's crib.

"Captain! Captain!" Kate screamed. She clutched Helen in her arms.

Helen Keller: Leader Without Sight or Sound

Parlor of the Keller Home, Ivy Green, in Tuscumbia.

Rushing into the Little House, he found Kate standing by Helen's crib, shaking and frantic. "What's wrong?"

"It's Helen," she cried. "She's burning up. Fetch the doctor!"

Kate put Helen back into her cradle. She poured cool water into a basin and soaked a cloth in it. Tenderly, she bathed the young girl's forehead and sang a lullaby to quiet her.

Hush little baby, don't say a word. Mamma's gonna buy you a mockingbird. As she sang, tears streamed down her cheeks.

The cold February wind howled outside, and Kate

watched eagerly for any sign of the doctor. After what seemed like an eternity, she heard horse hoofs approaching. Kate ran to the door and hurried the doctor inside.

I've been bathing her with cold water, but nothing I do seems to help. The fever won't go away.

The doctor opened his black bag and started his examination. *A fever's a dangerous thing, Mrs. Keller.*

Is it scarlet fever? Captain Keller asked.

Hard to say, the doctor replied. He sniffed Helen's mouth.

What are you doing? Kate asked.

In cases of scarlet fever, the patient usually has a sweet smell about their breath, he sighed. *I don't detect that with Helen.*

Then what is it? Kate demanded.

The doctor placed his hand on her shoulder. Mrs. Keller, *I think you need to prepare yourself. Looks like acute congestion of the stomach and brain.*

What can we do for that? Captain Keller asked impatiently.

With a grim expression, the doctor replied, *I'm afraid there is nothing to be done. The child will most likely die.*

Devastated, Kate and Captain Keller tried not to lose hope. Kate continued to apply cold washcloths to

Helen Keller: Leader Without Sight or Sound

Helen's head and body. Around the clock, Kate tirelessly tended to Helen not allowing her out of her sight for a second.

And as quickly as the fever came, it suddenly vanished. Even the doctor could not believe his eyes. *I have to tell you folks, I've never seen anything like it. A miracle. That's what it is. Simply a miracle.*

While Kate bathed Helen the next morning, she made a startling discovery. Her hand accidentally passed in front of the child's face, but Helen's eyelids didn't close.

Kate snapped her fingers in front of Helen's face. No response. She clapped her hands rapidly inches from Helen's eyes. The baby didn't blink or move. Her expressionless face sent a chill down Kate's spine.

Captain! she shrieked. Trembling, she clutched the frame of the cradle. *No. No. Please, God, no.*

Captain Keller rushed into the Little House. *What is it?*

Kate tried to speak, but the words were trapped in her throat. She pointed at Helen.

Kate? the Captain questioned. *She's fine. Helen's going to be fine. The doctor...*

Eyes, she mumbled. *She can't see.*

Instead of questioning her, Captain Keller waved his hands in front of Helen's face. No eye movement.

Darren J. Butler

The Kellers hurried Helen to an eye doctor in Union City, Tennessee. It was there that they learned Helen was blind. Heartbroken, they returned to Ivy Green only to make another shocking discovery.

Just before dinner, Helen was playing in the parlor near her crib. In the next room, the Keller's servant, Viney, rushed to make sure the table was properly set. Satisfied that everything was ready, she rang the dinner bell. The family made their way into the dining room to take their seats. But Helen did not come. Alarmed, Kate rang the bell again. Helen did not stir. Captain Keller and Kate rattled tin cans near her, but she did not react. They spoke to her gently, but Helen did not turn her head.

Helen Keller had slipped into a world of darkness and silence.

Helen Keller: Leader Without Sight or Sound

Spring, 1886

SHE IS NOT AN ANIMAL! Kate protested.

Captain Keller paced back and forth in front of the fireplace. *Kate, you mustn't let them upset you. They don't understand.*

Helen has just as much right to sit in that church on Sunday morning as anyone else, Kate pointed out.

My dear, Captain Keller replied calmly. *Her fits and tantrums are out of control. They disrupt the service.*

Kate glared at him. *She is not out of control, Captain. She wants to learn. She wants to see and to hear.*

Captain Keller sighed heavily. *Kate, you know that's not possible.*

Kate stood and crossed to the desk in the corner. She picked up the papers and brought them back to her husband. *Maybe it is,* she began. *Mr. Charles Dickens wrote about a girl in his American Notes. The girl's name was Laura Bridgman and her doctor, Dr. Howe, found a way to teach her.*

Darren J. Butler

I've read Mr. Dicken's account, Kate, he said. *But Dr. Howe is dead. Perhaps his work died with him. I don't see how the work of a man so far away could help our Helen.*

Kate did not give up so easily. *Perhaps. But what if it didn't?* She stepped away from the Captain and crossed the parlor to the window. *I just want our Helen to have a chance. I want her to see the sunshine and hear the chirp of the birds again. Don't you want that for our daughter?*

Captain Keller did not respond. She looked at him as he lowered his head. Kate looked out the window to see Helen playing with her dog, an old Irish Setter called Belle. In the cradle, baby Mildred was just starting to wake up from her nap. As Kate stared at their new infant, she was reminded of Helen when she was a baby.

No one realizes how smart she is. Almost six years old now and she lives every day of her life in a world of darkness and silence. But she wants to learn—she hungers to learn, Captain. She helps me fold the wash and put it away. She knows by the touch and the smell of our clothing where it belongs. The other day she locked me in the pantry for three hours because she was jealous of the baby.

And, she rocked Mildred out of her cradle and

Helen Keller: Leader Without Sight or Sound

almost...

She wasn't trying to hurt her, Captain, Kate insisted. *She was trying to let us know that she doesn't want to be forgotten. Helen understands that we use our voices to speak and our eyes to see. We owe it to her not to give up!*

A heavy silence fell over the room. Captain Keller watched Kate gazing out the window at the spring sunshine. *There is an oculist (a doctor who treats eye diseases) in Baltimore, Maryland that has done extraordinary things. I have heard that he has helped those that no one else could help. I'll take her to him if you want me to.*

A smile appeared on Kate's face. She simply nodded.

Captain Keller wrote to the doctor, and he agreed to see them. When the day finally came for them to leave, Aunt Ev decided to join the Captain and Helen on their journey.

Darren J. Butler

Meeting Dr. Bell

"ALL ABOARD!" the conductor called.

The final boarding call rang out across the platform, and the Captain, Helen and her Aunt Ev took their seats on the train, ready for the journey to Baltimore, Maryland. James and Simpson, Captain Keller's sons from his first marriage could take care of Ivy Green. Kate stayed behind to tend to Mildred, knowing that the trip would be too much for a baby to handle.

Helen sat quietly by the train window, the tips of her fingers gliding slowly over the glass. The morning sun had barely peeked over the horizon, but the warmth of its rays made the glass inviting to the tips of her fingers.

Very soon, Helen's attention turned to a rather peculiar doll that was placed on her lap. Crafted from large towels by her Aunt Ev, Helen fingered every inch of the doll with great curiosity. The face was blank, no features whatsoever, and a puzzled expression consumed Helen's tiny face.

Helen Keller: Leader Without Sight or Sound

What is it? Captain Keller asked. *Eveline. The last thing the child needs is more dolls, I...*

She needed a treat for the trip, Arthur, Aunt Ev replied matter of factly.

Suddenly, Helen's questioning hands found their way to her father's fingers. She grabbed them and placed them on the empty face of the doll. Tapping rapidly on the smooth surface, Helen's face yearned for an answer. When her father didn't reply immediately, Helen tapped her fingers to the doll's face and then to her own eyes. Over and over, she repeated the motions, growing more frustrated by the minute.

Giving up on her father for an answer, Helen grabbed Aunt Ev's hands and forced them to feel the doll too.

What's the matter with her? Captain Keller asked. *What does she want?*

A sullen expression came over Aunt Ev's face. *I didn't give the doll any eyes. My goodness. What was I thinking?* She reached into her bag and pulled out a needle and thread. *Arthur, I need the buttons from the sleeve of your coat.*

My buttons? he questioned. *Surely you don't think that Helen knows...*

Never mind! Aunt Ev said sternly, cutting her brother off. She started searching through her bag for anything she could use for eyes.

Helen wasn't about to give up. She too searched everything around her until her hands encountered beads on her aunt's cape. Excited, Helen jerked them off the cape and shoved them into the blank face of the doll.

Gently, Aunt Ev pulled them free of Helen's grasp and started sewing them in place. Helen waited patiently for her to finish. When her aunt presented the doll to her, Helen felt the eyes on the dolls face and then moved her fingers to her own eyes. A smile spread across Helen's face, and she clutched the doll to her chest.

Captain Keller watched the event with great interest. But his smiled faded quickly when he saw a tear roll down his daughter's cheek.

The train sped along the winding track towards Baltimore. By evening, Helen had made several friends up and down the aisle. Captain Keller watched her in a kind of awed silence as she tried to communicate with other people.

Amazing, he said at last.

What's that? Aunt Ev asked, not looking up from her knitting.

She is as calm as a lamb, he declared. *Not one tantrum or fit, and we've been cooped up in this com-*

Helen Keller: Leader Without Sight or Sound

partment for hours.

Aunt Ev stopped knitting and peered over the seat at Helen, who was now walking down the aisle with the conductor. He was teaching her how to punch the tickets of the passengers who boarded the train on the last stop.

The only time she breaks into those tantrums is when's she's bored, Aunt Ev said. *She wants to learn, Arthur. That's all she wants.*

I believe she can learn anything she wants.

If we find the right person to help her, Aunt Ev reminded him.

We will, Ev. We will, he said firmly.

Aunt Ev paused for a moment to think. *But Arthur. What if Dr. Chisholm can't help her? What if this blindness is irreversible?*

Captain Keller did not answer at once. Instead, he sat for several minutes studying Helen and the conductor going about their work. Finally, he broke his silence and spoke in a very determined tone.

If he says he can't help her, then we'll get another opinion and another after that if we have to.

What about this Dr. Howe we read about? Aunt Ev offered. *Surely his work with that Laura Bridgman girl could be helpful...*

Captain Keller broke his trance on Helen and

turned to Ev. *You're not giving up already, are you?*

She smiled. *No Arthur. I'm not giving up. But I am being realistic and so should you. If Dr. Chisholm says that nothing can be done, we need to find a teacher to help her.*

When the train arrived in Baltimore, it was a warm summer day. A carriage took Captain Keller, Aunt Ev, and Helen directly to Dr. Chisholm's office.

As they sat in the waiting room, Helen amused herself with a collection of shells that a nice lady on the train had given her. Captain Keller poked several holes in them, and Aunt Ev gave her a long piece of white yarn to string them. Patiently, Helen threaded each shell until she had a long necklace.

"Captain Keller?" the receptionist called. "Dr. Chisholm will see you now."

Captain Keller thanked her and led Helen into the doctor's office with Aunt Ev in their wake.

"I am Dr. Chisholm," the man said, holding out his hand.

"Thank you for seeing us. This is my sister, Ev, and this is Helen," said Captain Keller.

Dr. Chisholm bent down and held out his hand to Helen's face. As he touched her cheek, Helen felt his hand curiously. Her fingers moved up his arm to his face, where she greeted him by feeling his facial fea-

Helen Keller: Leader Without Sight or Sound

tures. He picked her up and sat her on the examination table.

For the next half hour, he examined her eyes. By the time he had finished, Dr. Chisholm's expression had not changed.

I'm sorry, Captain Keller, he began. *There is nothing that can be done for her eyes. The fever has robbed her of her sight and hearing forever.*

Captain Keller looked to Ev, who remained strong enough for both of them. She took her brother's hand and held it firmly.

Dr. Chisholm, please do not think me rude, the Captain said awkwardly. *Do you think we should get another opinion?*

Dr. Chisholm smiled. *Sir, I do not think you are being rude at all. If she were my child I would want the best for her. I would do everything in my power to restore her sight, but I'm afraid that all the opinions in the world cannot help her.*

Captain Keller shook his head slowly as he watched Helen playing with her shell necklace. This was not the news he had hoped for. He so wanted to go home and tell Kate that some of Helen's sight could be restored.

Dr. Chisholm lifted Helen off the examination table, and she wandered back to her aunt and father.

He slid a chair closer to them and took a seat.

Although her sight and hearing cannot be restored, I do think there is someone you should meet.

Captain Keller perked up. *Really? Who?*

Dr. Alexander Graham Bell will know of schools for blind and deaf children. It's the best thing for her and for you, he advised.

Ev spoke up, *Where is this Dr. Bell?*

He is in Washington, D.C., Dr. Chisholm replied. *I will be happy to make the arrangements for you.*

Ev looked to her younger brother, but his gaze focused only on Helen. She turned back to the doctor and answered him. *Make the arrangements, Dr. Chisholm. We will take the next train.*

The journey to Washington, D.C. was not very far. Within a few hours, they had arrived and searched the city for Dr. Bell's office. Ev could tell that her brother's heart was heavy. He had barely spoken a word during the trip from Baltimore.

Arthur, Ev said as they strolled down the city sidewalk.

Captain Keller did not respond. He continued walking, holding Helen's hand as they approached the next intersection.

Suddenly, Ev called out to him, *Arthur!*

Captain Keller stopped and turned around, his

Helen Keller: Leader Without Sight or Sound

brow crinkled. *What is it, Ev?*

Ev stood near the stone steps of an office building. *This is it! We've arrived at Dr. Bell's office!*

Although Ev tried to lift his spirits, Captain Keller barely acknowledged the fact that they had reached their destination. He stroked Helen's hair and looked up and down the street. Ev approached him and placed a firm hand on his shoulder.

Arthur Keller, she began. *Enough is enough. Having pity for her...wishing that some miracle is going to restore her sight and hearing is just not going to happen. The best thing you can do for your daughter is to march up those steps, meet this Dr. Bell, and find the best possible way to educate my niece. After all,* she is a Keller! *Members of the Keller family do not give up!*

A slight smile came across his face. The Captain took his sister's hand, kissed it properly and replied, *You're right, Ev. Kellers never give up.*

Inside, Dr. Bell greeted them warmly. As soon as they had entered his office, Helen took a liking to him. Before Captain Keller and Ev realized it, Helen had perched herself on Dr. Bell's lap and started fiddling with his pocket watch.

I'm sorry, Dr. Bell, Captain Keller said.

Don't be, he replied. *She is a very smart young lady. Please, tell me about her daily habits.*

Darren J. Butler

Well, Captain Keller began. *She has gestures...signs for things she wants.*

Go on...show me, Dr. Bell insisted.

She rubs her cheek when she wants her mother. Like this. Captain Keller stroked his cheek with his fingers. *For me, she pretends like she's putting on eye glasses. When she wants ice cream she acts like she's turning the ice cream churn and sometimes she holds her arms like she's cold.*

Excellent. Tell me more, Dr. Bell said.

Aunt Ev boasted, *Doctor, she can help her mother take the wash off the clothesline, fold them, and distribute them to the proper bedrooms in the house. She feels the fabric and smells...*

Yes. She's memorized how each person in your family smells as well as the touch of the fabric you wear. Quite extraordinary.

Captain Keller wanted to share in Dr. Bell's excitement, but he added, *However, at times she is simply out of control. We can't take her to church because she disturbs the congregation. She throws terrible tantrums when she doesn't get her way about things. My wife has to listen to our neighbors call her a wild animal. We just don't know what to do.*

Dr. Bell sat back his chair, the corners of his mouth rising into a grin. He patted young Helen on

Helen Keller: Leader Without Sight or Sound

the head and laughed. *Captain Keller. Believe me when I say, you have done very well in raising Helen.*

Captain Keller seemed confused. *Dr. Bell, didn't you hear what I said? She has no discipline. She runs wild and -*

And that is what has saved her my dear man, Dr. Bell began. *You see, in most cases, a blind and deaf child would have been locked away in some asylum. But instead of confining her, you allowed her to run free, to explore, to find her way in the world.*

Captain Keller's face brightened. *We simply didn't know what else to do.*

Dr. Bell laughed. *Indeed.*

But Ev had more that she wanted to share. *There's more, if you'd like to hear.*

Certainly, Dr. Bell replied eagerly. But as Aunt Ev spoke, Dr. Bell played with Helen, allowing her to make signs for him.

She loves flowers, Ev began. *She spends hours touching them and smelling them with not a single wild tendency. She follows her dog, an Irish Setter called Belle, around the estate, and they seem to have their own way of talking.*

Caught up in the moment, Captain Keller injected, *The estate is over six hundred acres, and we were having quite a problem with her roaming off, so I planted a large ring of boxwood shrubs next to the house. It's sort of like her play pen. She spends a great deal of time in there with her flowers and...*

But Captain Keller was interrupted by an outburst of laughter from Dr. Bell. He and Helen had engaged in a story of mimed motions. Helen's fingers explored Dr. Bell's hands as he communicated simple actions with her. He laughed once again at her playfulness and curiosity.

This is a delightful child, Dr. Bell said happily. *You must contact my friend, Mr. Anagnos immediately. He is the director of the Perkins Institution in Boston.*

Perkins? That is where Dr. Howe conducted his work, Ev injected.

Yes, that's correct, Dr. Bell replied. *You've heard of his work?*

We have, Ev replied. *Mr. Dicken's* American Notes *told all about Laura Bridgman...*

But Dr. Bell, Captain Keller interrupted. *Dr. Howe has been dead for many years. I know his work with that girl was amazing, but I can only wonder if his knowledge of how to educate a deaf and blind child died with him.*

Dr. Bell smiled and shook his head. *No, I assure you, it did not. Anagnos will know how to help Helen. I suggest you return to your fine home in Alabama and*

Helen Keller: Leader Without Sight or Sound

write to him. He would love to have Helen as a pupil.

No! Captain Keller exclaimed. *I cannot send her away to school. She's barely six years old.*

Helen's too young to be away from her parents. Surely you can see that, Aunt Ev injected.

Dr. Bell held up his hand to assure them. *Of course you are right. Perhaps Anagnos can send a teacher to Alabama.*

He wrapped his arms around Helen and gave her a hug before handing her over to Captain Keller and Ev. Crossing to his desk, he turned a page in a large, leather book. He scribbled down the address of the Perkins Institution and handed it to Captain Keller.

Thank you, Dr. Bell, Captain Keller said, shaking his hand.

You are very welcome, Dr. Bell replied. *I will eagerly wait to hear of Helen's progress.*

The wheels had been set in motion. When they returned home, Captain Keller wrote to Mr. Anagnos requesting his services. After a few weeks, the Kellers received a reply that a teacher had been found.

Almost nine months later, a young woman boarded a train in Boston to journey to Tuscumbia, Alabama. An eager, almost seven-year-old girl would finally meet the person who would deliver her from her world of blindness and deafness.

Darren J. Butler

Helen Keller and Dr. Alexander Graham Bell several years after their first meeting. (Photo from 1903 issue of Popular Science Monthly. *Courtesy of American Federation for the Blind.)*

Helen Keller: Leader Without Sight or Sound

The Endless Train Ride To Tuscumbia

SNOWFLAKES WHIRLED around Annie Sullivan and Mrs. Hopkins as they stood waiting for the horse and carriage. Annie's hands shook, and she tried to steady them.

Cold dear? Mrs. Hopkins asked.

No, Annie replied simply. *I must admit...I'm nervous.*

Mrs. Hopkins took Annie's hands into her own. *Don't be. You'll be a wonderful teacher.*

"*Will I?* she asked doubtfully. *I'm sure my teachers at Perkins are laughing in their sleeve at the thought of Annie Mansfield Sullivan being a teacher.*

Mrs. Hopkins smiled. *I'm sure you're wrong.*

Annie laughed. "Really? One of them asked me what I liked about the art of teaching. Do you know what I told her?"

A worried expression came across Mrs. Hopkins face. *I'm afraid to ask.*

"I said *'Nothing.'*"

Mrs. Hopkins sighed and shook her head. *Annie. You must avoid saying things like this. Other people will not understand...especially people in the South, will not understand your ways.*

Annie cleared her throat and adjusted the red ribbons holding on her gray bonnet. Silence fell between them for several moments. In the distance, Annie could see the horse and carriage approaching.

When you refer to other people, you mean the Kellers? Annie asked.

Mrs. Hopkins nodded.

Mrs. Hopkins. Her voice was now softer, almost apologetic. *I promise you that I will be as ladylike as possible. I understand the importance of my work with this child.*

At that moment, Mr. Anagnos appeared from around the corner, rushing to catch up with them.

Ah! There you are! he exclaimed. *My brightest pupil!*

Annie turned sharply to him with raised eyebrows. This would be the last time she would see the rotund, Greek man for quite some time. He had been the

Helen Keller: Leader Without Sight or Sound

closest thing to a parent to her in the years she had spent at Perkins. Although they didn't agree most of the time, she had a great affection for him.

If I'm so bright, then why have you delayed this journey for seven months?

Mr. Anagnos put a heavy hand on her shoulder. *I wanted you to be ready, Annie. This is a difficult undertaking, and it should not be taken lightly.*

The carriage stopped and the three of them stepped inside. Once they were settled, Annie resumed their conversation.

I don't take anything lightly. You of all people should know that, Mr. Anagnos.

He laughed heartily. *No, of course not. Do you have everything you need?*

Yes. I have some kindergarten beads and cards, two or three Braille readers, and a Braille slate ...

Even though Helen was not ready for them, Annie hoped that at some point her young student would be ready to read. Many of the children's early readers had been translated into braille. As soon as a child was ready to read, their teacher would introduce the books filled with raised bumps instead of printed words. Once a child learned the raised symbols for each letter, they could string them together into words and then sentences.

Good! Mr. Anagnos interrupted.

Michael, Mrs. Hopkins said gently. *You are changing the subject. Listen to her.*

Of course, he replied.

Annie gathered her thoughts. *Ever since last August when you sent me Captain Keller's letter, I've been thinking about this day. For seven months now I've read and re-read every word that Dr. Howe wrote about his work with Laura Bridgman and the others.*

Mr. Anagnos nodded. *I know, Annie. You have worked feverishly to prepare, and I'm proud of you.*

I haven't done anything yet.

You will, Mrs. Hopkins added. *If anyone can understand what this child is going through, it's you.*

Annie gazed up at the falling snow. *I never thought my own blindness would help me.*

It will, Mr. Anagnos said firmly. *After nine operations on your eyes, you can empathize with this girl.*

Oh, and you must remember to wash them out daily as the doctor prescribed, Mrs. Hopkins injected.

I will, Annie replied.

They climbed aboard the carriage and pulled the door shut. For several blocks they rode with only the sounds of the carriage and the noises of the street. There was a question lingering in Annie's mind that she wanted to ask Mr. Anagnos. As they drew closer to

Helen Keller: Leader Without Sight or Sound

the train station, she knew that this would be the last opportunity.

Mr. Anagnos? she asked.

Yes, Annie.

When you corresponded with Captain Keller...did you tell him about my past?

No, her teacher said gently.

This was the answer Annie had hoped for. She would tell them on her own terms. The less they knew, the better.

Annie looked Mr. Anagnos square in the eye and said, *Thank you.*

It is your past, Annie, he reminded her. *It is your decision who you choose to share it with.*

Annie's life had been a tough one.

A disease called trachoma, caused by a bacteria that attacks her eyes, went untreated. Because of that she was almost blind.

Her family had been one of the poorest in Massachusetts. Her father was a drunk and when her mother died when Annie was nine years old, she and her brother Jimmie were sent to live at the Tewksbury Almshouse, a place for the poor, the disabled and the mentally ill.

Little Jimmie suffered a tubercular hip, a painful

inflammation of the hip joint. The disease weakened his small body and he died only a few months after arriving at Tewksbury.

It was a terrible place for anyone to be, especially a little girl all alone and nearly blind. The people there were cruel. Annie had no childhood happiness; it was all she could do just to survive.

The head of the nearby Perkins School for the Blind was asked to investigate reports of cruelty at Tewksbury. During that investigation, the investigator discovered little Annie and asked that she be released to the Perkins School.

Authorities at Tewksbury agreed. Annie missed her brother Jimmie terribly, but proved to be an excellent student at Perkins. She also had a number of operations on her eyes and by the time she was a teenager, she could see again!

It has been a long and hard road from blindness and cruelty at Tewksbury to becoming a tough, hard working, outspoken and excellent student at Perkins.

Annie looked at Mr. Anagnos and bit her bottom lip. With a quiver in her voice, she said, *Annie. Jimmie used to call me that. It reminds me of...*

I know, Mr. Anagnos said. *I know you miss him very much. I see it in your eyes.*

Helen Keller: Leader Without Sight or Sound

Annie nodded. *They say the eyes are the gateway to the soul.*

That they are, my dear. That they are.

The carriage stopped in front of the Boston train station. Mr. Anagnos and Mrs. Hopkins helped Annie to the train platform with her trunk and bag. The snow had started to fall more heavily by the time they boarded the train. The porter greeted them and showed Annie to her seat.

Now, when it is time for bed, the porter will come and show you how your seat turns into your bed, Mr. Anagnos instructed.

And I suggest you rise early to take care of your toiletries, Mrs. Hopkins added.

The train whistle blew long and hard. The conductor walked down the aisle calling for all passengers to be seated.

We have to go, Mr. Anagnos said.

Write to us, Annie, and let us know how you're getting along, Mrs. Hopkins pleaded.

I will! Annie said excitedly. *I'll send you all of my notes on Helen's progress!*

Mr. Anagnos and Mrs. Hopkins left the train quickly and stood on the platform to watch the train depart. With her face pressed to glass, Annie watched them fade away as the train gathered up steam and barreled down the tracks.

For the first time, Annie felt alone. She had never ridden a train before and didn't know how to order a meal or what to ask for. Mrs. Hopkins had packed her a lunch, but when she took it out the porter appeared at her side at once.

May I get you a table, Miss? he asked.

A table? Annie thought. *How in the world could a table fit in such a small space?*

That would be fine, Annie replied finally.

When he set up the table with a tablecloth, Annie was amazed at the clever arrangement.

Would you like coffee or tea? the porter asked.

Coffee, please.

The porter returned shortly with a tray containing a small silver pot of steaming hot coffee with cream and sugar in a silver pitcher and bowl. Annie was a bit disturbed thinking about the cost of such extravagance.

A little later, the porter returned and directed Annie to a seat near the end of the car where an old lady was sitting. He explained to Annie that she must wait there until her bed was ready.

Annie took notice of the old lady who seemed fidgety, fussy, and inquisitive.

Was that man who brought you aboard your father? the old lady asked.

Helen Keller: Leader Without Sight or Sound

No, he was my teacher at school, Annie replied hesitantly.

I see. And the lady? Was that his wife?

No. Just a friend.

Where are you going? Washington, D.C.? the lady questioned.

No. I'm going to Alabama, Annie replied, trying to be patient with the woman.

The lady gasped, *Whatever for?*

Annie grew a bit afraid. Why was this lady asking her so many questions?

I'm going there to be a private teacher to a girl, and...

But the woman jumped in and didn't let Annie speak again. She went on and on about her life and her family. Annie could not believe how much she told her in such a short time.

When the porter returned to tell Annie that her bed was ready, she was relieved to leave the woman. At the same time, the porter was checking tickets, but the lady could not produce hers! She had lost it and fumbled about her clothing in search of it. Giggling to herself, Annie walked down the aisle to her bed. The porter showed her how to seal up the curtain, and Annie settled in for a night's rest.

The next morning, Annie woke to a great shock.

She had missed her connection and the train headed for Alabama was long gone by an hour at least. She was stuck in Washington, D.C.!

When will the next train leave? Annie asked.

Tomorrow morning, he replied matter of factly.

Annie's heart beat fast, and she felt dizzy, her mind a blank. The porter summoned a gentleman to help her. In her dazed state, Annie was introduced to Mr. Rider, a teacher in Washington, D.C.

Perhaps you should check into a hotel and wait for tomorrow's train, he suggested.

Embarrassed, Annie admitted, *I've never checked into a hotel before. I don't know how.*

I will go with you and attend to everything if you wish, Mr. Rider answered.

Annie detected a bit of nuisance in his voice, but she had no other choice. The porter gathered up her belongings and they proceeded to the doors leading out of the train station.

Would you like a taxi or should we take a street car? Mr. Rider asked. *The street car passes the hotel.*

The porter injected, *I suggest the taxi sir. She has a trunk as well.*

Very well, Mr. Rider announced. *We shall take the taxi.*

Worried at how much the taxi would cost, Annie

Helen Keller: Leader Without Sight or Sound

hesitated but realized she was in little position to argue. Momentarily, the horse and carriage pulled up to the curb and the porter loaded her trunk. Annie climbed aboard and Mr. Rider silently took the seat opposite her.

When they arrived at the Riggs Hotel, Mr. Rider registered for her and suggested that she might like something to eat. Thankful for his assistance, Annie asked Mr. Rider if he would accompany her into the dining room.

Mr. Rider agreed and he asked for a quiet table. During the meal, Annie noticed that Mr. Rider relaxed, and she enjoyed the conversation about his school. He seemed quite surprised that she was making such a long journey alone at her age of twenty.

After lunch, Mr. Rider asked Annie if she would like to see the White House and some of the state buildings. Annie went with pleasure! Although she felt the part of the country cousin, Annie accompanied Mr. Rider dressed in a plain, dark blue dress with large buttons down the front. She wore a small bonnet fastened under her chin with a red bow. Around her shoulders she wore a cape of the same material as the dress, lined with a light gray.

The day was warm, and her high-buttoned shoes started to hurt her feet terribly. Mr. Rider suggested that she take off her cape, and he carried it for her along their tour of the city. They walked around White House and looked at the Treasury Building, but Annie was miserable and couldn't enjoy herself.

Unable to stand the pain any longer, she said, *Mr. Rider, if you don't mind, I think I should like to go back to the hotel. My shoes are hurting my feet, and I'm not sure I can walk another step.*

Of course, Mr. Rider replied.

In fact, Annie felt as though he was relieved to end the tour of the city. Mr. Rider accompanied her back to the hotel and told Annie that he would come for her the next morning and take her to the train station.

Sleep well, Miss Sullivan. You should be ready to leave the hotel by nine o'clock.

Annie thanked him, and as he walked away, she reveled at the name he had called her. "Miss Sullivan." It made her feel like she was all grown up!

After Annie bathed her feet in cold water and washed her face, she laid down across her bed and sobbed herself to sleep.

When she woke, it was pitch dark. Annie stumbled about the room trying to find the light. She sat on the side of her bed wondering helplessly what she should do. Annie went to the door and looked out

Helen Keller: Leader Without Sight or Sound

into the hallway to see if she could find a maid, but the hallway was empty. To her surprise, Annie found the key to her hotel room in the keyhole outside! She remembered how Mrs. Hopkins had strictly warned her to keep track of her hotel key. Annie retreated into her room and locked the door behind her. Clutching the key in her palm, she laid down on the bed again. She felt hungry and suddenly remembered her lunch basket. Sitting in the dark, she ate the sandwiches and pickles, salting them with her own tears.

Annie took off her dress and crawled into bed, trying to get hold of her feelings. In a matter of minutes, she drifted off to sleep.

Sometime during the night, Annie woke with an intense pain in the eye Dr. Derby had operated on only a few days before she left Boston. Her tears had irritated the eye, and it was swelling. She made a compress of a wet towel for her eye and fell asleep again.

The next morning, the bright rays of sunlight poured through the window and revived Annie's courage. Mr. Rider collected her at nine o'clock and before she knew it, Annie found herself on the train once more hoping that the worst part of her adventure had come to an end.

Annie gazed out the window at Virginia. The pale

blue sky hovered over a beautiful spring day. A blue haze lingered over the mountains almost hiding them like a sweet secret.

As the train barreled south down the tracks, Annie began to see black people. They passed a cabin with a large black woman with a red bandanna wound around her head, standing in the doorway watching the train go by. A black boy down a dirt path balancing a large basket on his head like a cap. Small black children with fuzzy pigtails threw stones into a creek, taking a moment to wave to the train gleefully.

These round about tickets create a long journey, don't they?

Annie looked up to see the conductor in the aisle beside her.

"The man who sold me this ticket ought to be hanged, and I'll be happy to act as hangman!" Annie exclaimed.

Those are the Blue Ridge Mountains, he added. *I s'pose you have heard of 'em.*

Not until this moment, Annie laughed.

The conductor tipped his hat and proceeded down the aisle stopping every now and then to speak to the passengers.

The train stopped in Lynchburg, Virginia for about an hour. The conductor led a small group of passengers on a walking tour. The town was hilly and the street perpendicular. Annie saw mules that were the most bedraggled animals she had ever seen.

Once they boarded the train, the conductor assured her that there would be no more changes between there and Tuscumbia. Annie took her seat, and the porter was kind enough to bring her a bowl of cracked ice and plenty of towels to tend to her swollen eye.

The next day they reached Tennessee. Annie was astonished at how muddy the river was. To her, the countryside seemed poor. The dirt was red, and Annie thought it had a rare, warm beauty about it. She mar-

The Tuscumbia train station where the Kellers met Miss Sullivan.

veled at the Negro cabins, which were so dilapidated, it brought tears to her eyes.

By the time the train finally stopped in Tuscumbia, Alabama, the ache in Annie's heart was sharper than the pain in her eye. She longed for her friends in Boston. To Annie, Perkins had never seemed like home—until this very moment.

Helen Keller: Leader Without Sight or Sound

Student Meets Teacher

MARCH 3, 1887

As Annie entered the train platform, she heard a single voice calling her name.

"Miss Sullivan?"

A young man in his early twenties looked at her questioningly. Before another word was spoken, an odd feeling consumed Annie. As she looked upon him, she realized that they would never be friends.

"I'm James Keller," he said.

James. Her little brother was named James, though she called him Jimmie. An icy pain raced down her spine as she reached out to shake the gentleman's hand.

"I'm Annie Sullivan." These were the only words she could manage.

"Captain Keller and his wife are waiting in the carriage," he said matter of factly.

His wife. Annie made a note of his reference to Mrs. Keller. Obviously, the woman was not his mother, and Annie detected resentment in his tone.

"What about Helen?" Annie asked.

"She's home. It's not far," James said. He motioned to a set of stairs that led to the road.

Captain Keller and Kate Keller were waiting in the carriage. A small crowd had gathered near the carriage to see the Yankee girl who was going to teach the Keller girl. Annie felt their stares at her felt shoes and swollen eye.

Slowly, Annie approached the carriage. Captain Keller and Kate hesitantly descended to the ground.

Miss Sullivan? I'm Captain Keller and this is my wife Mrs. Kate Keller.

Hello, Captain Keller. I'm happy to meet you both, Annie replied timidly.

James heaved Annie's trunk into the back of the carriage. Without a word, he climbed aboard and waited impatiently.

I see you've met my eldest son, James, Captain Keller said.

Annie nodded. *Yes, we met on the platform. Is your home far from here?*

Just up the road, Kate said, pointing down a dirt path.

57

Helen Keller: Leader Without Sight or Sound

Ivy Green, the Keller home in Tuscumbia, where Miss Sullivan soon arrived after a short ride from the train station.

"Shall I push the horse?" Annie suggested.

Her dry humor was not met with laughter from the Kellers. Instead, Captain Keller offered his hand to help her into the carriage. Once they were all aboard, the small crowd departed, and Captain Keller steered the horse and carriage down the dirt road.

Eagerly, Annie sat on the edge of her seat as the Keller home came into view. In the distance, she could see a small figure standing in the doorway of the house. The carriage came to a halt, and Annie scrambled out of her seat.

As she approached the front porch, Annie saw her

pupil. Helen's brown hair was tumbled, her dress soiled, and her black shoes tied with white strings. Annie stopped in her tracks, and an overwhelming feeling consumed her.

Later that day Annie would write in her journal:

"The moment I beheld that eager, pathetic little face, I knew my fate was sealed. Henceforth I should belong to her. There would be no release until death parted us. That little Helen would take the place of my brother Jimmie, the only thing in my life I had deeply loved."

Annie whispered to herself, "O God, may I be found equal to my task."

Suddenly, Helen realized that her family had returned. She tumbled off the steps exploring each person until she encountered Annie. If Captain Keller had not been standing behind Annie, the force of Helen's actions would have surely toppled Annie to the ground.

Annie reached out to touch Helen's face, but the young girl diverted Annie's efforts to embrace her or kiss her. Instead, Helen jerked Annie's bag away from her and threw a tantrum when Kate tried to get it back. Annie stepped in and presented Helen with her pocket watch. Curious of the object, Helen calmed down and led Annie into the house and up the stairs

Helen Keller: Leader Without Sight or Sound

to the bedroom that awaited her.

As she crossed into the house, Annie caught a glimpse of Kate Keller moving towards her, and Captain Keller stopping her.

The room was small and simple. Sunlight shone in from the window and illuminated the bright white spread covering the four-poster bed. A writing desk sat in one corner. Helen laid Annie's bag on the bed and started exploring its contents. She seemed quite disappointed to only find toiletries and a few articles of clothing. As she encountered the bottom of the bag, Helen put her hand to her mouth and shook her head with great emphasis. She gave up interest in the bag and wandered into the hallway.

Annie found her crouched beside a trunk. She moved quickly to the child and tried to use Helen's signs to tell her that she had a trunk just like it with something good to eat inside. Helen put her hands to her mouth and went through the motions of eating something delicious. Annie's eyes grew large with interest and excitement. Behind those blank, still eyes was a mind eager to learn. Helen pointed once again to the trunk and nodded vigorously as if to tell Annie that she understood about the food that waited for her inside of Annie's trunk. Helen stood and scampered down the stairs with Annie on her heels.

The moment her little feet hit the floor of the ground level, Helen started sniffing in search of someone. Her mother sat in the parlor across the hall with an anxious expression. As Helen scrambled to wrap her arms around her, Kate looked to Annie for some sign of hope.

Excited, Helen repeated the motions about the trunk and food to eat, telling her mother of her discovery. A cautious smile spread across Kate's face. Looking to Annie once again, she saw the teacher smiling as well.

Later that evening, just before bed, Annie gave Helen the doll that the girls from Perkins School for the Blind had purchased for her. She rubbed Helen's fingers against the doll and made letters in Helen's palm. "D...o...l...l. Doll, Helen. This is a doll. D...o...l...l."

Taking one letter at a time, she showed Helen how to form each letter with her fingers. Curious of this finger game, Helen played along not realizing that she was spelling a word. Annie repeated the word several times, and each time Helen spelled it back. Each time she spelled it correctly, Annie placed Helen's hand on her own cheek and nodded to signal, "Yes."

"Now, if I could only make you understand that

Helen Keller: Leader Without Sight or Sound

those letters spell doll and that this is a doll."

Annie's fear that Helen would be incapable of learning the manual alphabet was washed away. She gave Helen the doll and led her to the small bedroom next to her own. Mrs. Keller was there to tuck her in.

As Annie stepped back into her bedroom, a sense of relief came over her. The first lesson had been a success.

Darren J. Butler

The Spoiled Child

THE NEXT MORNING, Annie awoke to streams of sunlight bouncing off her face. She reached to the nightstand for her glasses to shield her weak eyes. A fresh spring aroma trickled in from the open window, and Annie listened to the birds singing their sweet melodies. This was a far cry from the hustle and bustle of the Boston streets. Annie laid there for several moments taking in the quiet.

Downstairs, muffled voices lashed back and forth. One filled with anger and the other whimsical. Occasionally, another younger voice chimed in, but it was always followed by an abrupt burst of laughter. Curious to know what they were talking about, Annie dressed quickly, checking herself in the mirror before heading downstairs.

As she reached the bottom step, the muffled voices became distinct. Captain Keller was in a heated discussion with his eldest son, James, over the outcome of the Civil War. Simpson, the younger son,

Helen Keller: Leader Without Sight or Sound

chimed in every now and then with a sarcastic comment that left Captain Keller fuming.

The moment Annie stepped into the dining room, the conversation ceased. All three of them rose.

Miss Sullivan. We were afraid you had overslept, Captain Keller said.

James pulled out one of the vacant chairs and waited for Annie to take her seat. She nodded at him and smiled as she sat down to breakfast.

I didn't realize how exhausted I was from the journey, Annie explained. *I'm not sure when I've had a sounder sleep.*

Kate placed her hand on top of Annie's. *I'm glad to hear it, Miss Sullivan. The country atmosphere must be refreshing to you.*

Oh it is, Annie replied. *I must admit, I had no idea how quiet the mornings...*

Quiet? James said amused. *Miss Sullivan, it is never quite around Ivy Green as long as there's a lively discussion about the War Between the States.*

Civil War, Simpson injected.

Captain Keller's eyebrows raised in objection. *Simpson. In this house, we refer to the war as the War Between the States.*

Simpson chuckled. *Yes, father.*

A heavy silence fell over the table. Annie thought

about several ways to join the conversation. The Gettysburg Address. The assassination of President Lincoln. None of these topics seemed like discussions she wanted to have with Captain Keller at the moment. She observed that the Captain's sons enjoyed poking at him about the Civil War. It seemed to rile this normally gentle man. But after all, Captain Keller had served proudly in the Confederate Army. She was certain that he had many feelings about the men he had served with, losses, and the ultimate surrender.

Annie decided to steer the conversation another direction.

I was quite impressed with Helen's first lesson last evening.

Lesson? Captain Keller asked.

Why yes, Annie replied. *Helen seems to be very intelligent. She's a quick learner and eager.*

Captain Keller put his fork down and leaned back in his chair. Rubbing his chin whiskers, he asked again, *What lesson?*

Annie turned to Mrs. Keller. *Didn't you tell him?*

Kate set down her cup and looked to Captain Keller. *I told you, Captain. Remember? Helen realized there was something in Miss Sullivan's trunk.*

Captain Keller sighed. *And you call that a lesson? Please elaborate, Miss Sullivan.*

Helen Keller: Leader Without Sight or Sound

All eyes stared at her. *Well, I needed to find out how she learns. Some children like Helen are unwilling to learn. I wanted to size her up and find out what kind of student I had.*

I see. Go on, Captain Keller urged.

To begin with, Helen realized you were expecting a guest. Mrs. Keller told me that Helen had been exploring the room for days. With fresh linens and the window open to let in the fresh air, Helen knew that the room was being prepared for a guest. When I arrived, you saw her there on the front steps exploring my face, my hands...and then she led me to that room. That's brilliant on her part.

I could probably train our dog to do the same thing, Simpson said.

Captain Keller cleared his throat, and Simpson wiped the smirk off his face. He noted Kate's disfavor as well. Annie didn't miss a beat.

Yes, I'm sure you could, Simpson. That is exactly what I have to do with Helen. Train her.

Like a dog? James asked. *That seems barbaric Miss Sullivan.*

Babies are trained. They start out by observing others. Listening to the tones of our voice to know if their parents are happy or unhappy...

I'm sorry to interrupt you Miss Sullivan, but Helen

is blind and deaf. She doesn't have the advantages that other children do, Captain Keller said.

Kate could no longer stay quiet. *But she did, Captain. Before the fever, she was a bright, eager child. She took her first steps on her first birthday. She could say several words. Mama. Papa. Cup. Dog. Water and many more. Until that wretched fever took her sight and hearing away from her, Helen was just like any other baby.*

Annie nodded. *That's what I'm counting on. All of that knowledge is locked inside of her. I just have to find a way to let it out. Once she learns how to communicate with me, I'll be able to...*

Communicate? Simpson asked with a laugh. *Do you mean she'll be able to talk?*

Yes, it's possible, Annie answered.

How can she do that if she can't hear what we're saying? James asked.

First, I must teach her what a word is. I have to make her understand that everything has a name. I'll start with the manual alphabet." Annie held up her fist and made the letter A.

Everyone around the table stared at her balled up fist. Kate imitated the movement, and Annie nodded at her.

I've read about the manual alphabet, Kate said

Helen Keller: Leader Without Sight or Sound

excitedly.

Simpson shook his head. *I don't see how she's gonna learn a bunch of hand motions when she can't even see them.*

She'll feel them, Simpson. I'll teach Helen everything by touch. We started last evening with a doll the girls from my school sent to her.

Annie waited for the next question, but no one said a word. Mrs. Keller seemed excited and eager, but Captain Keller sat back in his chair with a not-so-sure expression on his face. The boys seemed amused by Annie's plan of action to teach their stepsister.

Just as Annie was about to lecture them on Dr. Howe's research, Helen wandered into the room sniffing. The aromas of Viney's cooking had caught her attention, and she felt her way to the table. Suddenly, Annie realized that there wasn't a place set for Helen. Before she could voice this, Helen's hand plunged into her mother's plate. Stunned, Annie gaped at the sight of the little slobbery hands grabbing food from the plate and shoving it into her mouth. When Helen had her fill from one plate, she proceeded to the next. Her brothers were less tolerant of their spoiled little sister and tried to push her away. Helen continued around the table until she reached her father's plate. Once again, she ate her fill without any resistance. Annie

Darren J. Butler

The Keller dining room, scene of Helen's fit.

was dumbfounded that Helen's parents were allowing her to behave that way.

Annie glared at the little waif as she rounded the corner of the table and headed for her own plate. As Helen's fingertips felt the lace tablecloth and encountered the edge of Annie's plate, her hands also encountered something quite different. In a swift move, Annie grabbed hold of Helen's wrists and jerked them away from the table.

Miss Sullivan? What are you doing? Captain Keller asked.

I will not let this spoiled child upset my plate! Annie exclaimed.

Helen Keller: Leader Without Sight or Sound

Spoiled child? Captain Keller fired back. *Now see here, Miss Sullivan.*

Helen began to kick and try to free herself from Annie's hold, but Annie wrapped her arms around the child and pulled her close.

Miss Sullivan, please. We let her eat from our plates because she can't sit still, Kate explained.

Mrs. Keller, Helen needs to learn how to sit still and eat with a spoon like a little lady, Annie said.

James and Simpson burst into laughter. Captain Keller stood and raised his hand to quiet them.

Miss Sullivan, he began in a more controlled, gentle tone. *I understand that you are not accustomed to a child eating from your plate, but I do not see the harm. Now if you will kindly let her go, I'm sure we can...*

Captain Keller! Annie interrupted. *Helen must be disciplined before any learning can begin. Now, if all of you will leave us alone, I will teach her some manners.*

Kate jumped from her seat and tried to pull Helen from Annie's grasp. Annie tightened her grip and pulled her away from her mother.

Miss Annie, please, Kate pleaded.

Annie paused. *Mrs. Keller, surely you understand that a child must be disciplined. Just last night you told me about her unruliness in church and how the people of this community call her a wild animal. What did you tell me?*

Tears trickled down Kate's cheeks. *I don't like it. Helen is not a wild animal. She just can't sit still and...*

Then let me teach her how. Don't you see? She's not being wild. She's trying to learn. She's curious. She wants to know about the world around her...the world that was taken away from her. Annie waited for a response from the Kellers. No one moved. Even Helen seemed frozen in her arms waiting for the next action. *I beg of you to leave this room at once and allow me to teach her. That is what you hired me to do. Please let me do my job.*

Without a word, Captain Keller crossed the room to the door and waited for his sons and wife make their exit. As Kate and the boys walked out of the room, Captain Keller locked eyes with Annie for a moment. Although he didn't speak a word, Annie felt that he understood what had to be done. He followed his wife and sons into the hallway and out the front door.

The Fight

ANNIE TURNED HELEN LOOSE and locked the door that led into the hallway as well as the one that led into the parlor. Helen remained motionless. When her mother didn't scoop her up, Helen started feeling her way around the table. With each empty chair she discovered, Helen became more agitated. By the time she reached the last chair, her outrage turned into a tantrum. She fell to the floor and started kicking and pounding the floor with her fists.

Annie watched the tantrum for several moments and then walked back to her own chair. Ready for the tantrum to end, Annie picked up her chair and banged it against the floor. Helen felt the wave of vibrations and her kicking slowed to a stop.

Helen sat up and began sniffing the room. She felt her way around the table again. When her fingertips encountered Annie's arm, Helen pulled away quickly. Cautiously, she touched her arm again, realizing that the arm was in the motion of doing something. Helen followed the action until she realized that Annie was eating her scrambled eggs. Helen plunged her hand into Annie's plate. Annie slapped the little hand, and Helen took a step back.

Not willing to give up so easily, Helen dropped to the floor. She grabbed the chair legs and tried to yank the chair out from underneath Annie! Startled, Annie almost choked on her eggs. Instead of confronting her, Annie sat more firmly in the chair, unwilling to let the little Helen topple her again. Frustrated that Annie hadn't moved, Helen tried to yank the chair once again, but this time she met resistance. Both girls held their own in a sort of tug of war game until Helen gave up, more agitated than before.

Helen slid her hand over Annie's dress until she found her thigh. In one swift movement, Helen pinched it. Without thinking, Annie slapped the little hand. Helen pinched her again. Annie slapped harder. Helen sat back, trying to decide what to do. Annie watched her closely for a few moments before returning to her breakfast.

Soon, she felt the gentle touch of Helen's hand exploring the bottom of her dress, then the waist, and slowly up the arm. The tiny fingers found Annie's cheek and followed her chewing motion. Without warning, Helen struck Annie across the face. Annie's

Helen Keller: Leader Without Sight or Sound

hand backslapped Helen across her face. Helen slapped Annie. Annie slapped Helen. The young girl reared back to deliver another blow, but froze in her back-swing. Not wanting to lose the battle, Helen squeezed out an animalistic cry of frustration. The growl-like moan was the first emotional sound Annie had heard from Helen. But she didn't feel pity. Instead, she smiled. Helen's emotional response to the battle showed strategic thinking on her part. In other words, she was far smarter than anyone realized.

After several moments of no movement, Helen took off on all fours around the table until she found her mother's chair. Crawling into the chair, Helen swiped the back of her hand against her face over and over. This was her sign for "mother."

She's not here! Annie bellowed. She grabbed the little hand and tried to spell mother into it, but Helen bit her instead.

Helen scrambled out of the chair and tried to run toward one of the doors. Tumbling over chairs and colliding with the edge of the fireplace, Helen ran into the door with a thud. She banged and kicked at the door, pleading for anyone to let her out. Annie grabbed her wrists and dragged her back into a chair, but Helen sprang from the seat and headed towards the other door. Annie caught her just as she started banging on the door. Once again, she dragged her wiggling body back to the chair.

After planting Helen firmly in the chair, Annie scooted it up to the table and attempted to put a spoon in her hand. Helen refused to hold the spoon and sunk into the chair until she was under the table! She crawled to the other side, but Annie was there to scoop her up. This time, Helen kicked harder and flailed so hard that Annie almost dropped her. The second that Annie put her down in the chair, Helen leaped onto the table and crawled across like a lightning bolt! Annie ran around the table and caught Helen before she crawled off the table.

Helen's body was rigid, filled with anger and frustration. Her cheeks were as red and hot as fire. She noticed tears trickling down her cheeks, but Annie refused to feel pity for her. This was a battle she planned to win!

Once Annie placed Helen back in her chair, she waited for her to bolt. But this time, Helen didn't move an inch. She sat still, seemingly exhausted. Panting and trying to catch her breath, Annie waited for Helen to react, but she didn't. Cautiously, Annie picked up a spoon and tried to put it in her hand. Without emotion, Helen refused to grip the spoon's handle. Her hand remained as limp as a noodle. The spoon fell to

Helen Keller: Leader Without Sight or Sound

the tablecloth.

Annie tried again, but Helen didn't grip it. A third time, Annie attempted to make Helen hold the spoon. When Helen didn't comply, Annie closed Helen's tiny fingers around the spoon's handle. She scooped up some scrambled eggs and brought them close to Helen's mouth. Just as the spoon met Helen's lips, she threw the spoon across the room where it hit the wall. Annie put another spoon in Helen's hand and tried again. Once again, Helen threw the spoon across the room, hitting the door.

Refusing to surrender, Annie grabbed Helen around her middle and dragged her across the room to where the spoon lay. Annie forced her to grab hold of the spoon and returned her to her seat.

As the spoonful of eggs touched her lips, Helen defiantly threw the spoon again. Annie snatched her up and dragged her to where the spoon lay near the china cabinet. But this time, Helen had allowed her entire body to go limp. Just as Annie placed her hand on the spoon, Helen pushed Annie off of her sending the teacher hurling against the wall. Helen scurried across the room, toppling chairs in her wake to keep Annie from catching up with her. Once Helen located her own chair, she sat firmly and grabbed hold of the seat's edge.

Darren J. Butler

Annie stood in amazement across the room. Helen had created an obstacle course of chairs to keep her from pursuit, and now she had a death grip on the chair! Taking her time, Annie picked up the chairs in her path and sat them upright in their place. She walked around Helen contemplating her next move. The seven year old seemed determined not to move from this chair again.

Annie grabbed Helen's left hand and pried her fingers from the chair. Helen allowed it to hang loose, and Annie proceeded to the other hand. As quickly as Annie freed the right hand, Helen grabbed both side of the chair once again! Unwilling to play this game with her, Annie picked up the chair and shook it until Helen let go and toppled into the floor. She picked her up, deposited her back in the chair and placed another spoon in her hand.

As expected, Helen hurled the spoon across the room. Since making her pick up the spoons didn't seem to be working, Annie grabbed a handful of spoons from the buffet. One after another, Annie put a spoon in Helen's hand, and Helen threw it across the room. After the fifth spoon toss, Annie decided to *make* Helen throw the spoons! Faster and faster Annie loaded Helen's hand with spoon after spoon and made her throw them. Finally, Helen grew tired of throwing

Helen Keller: Leader Without Sight or Sound

spoons and held onto one in the air. She shook it above her head and made an excited sound that was low and seemed to come from the back of her throat.

Feeling like she had gotten her point across, Annie proceeded with trying to make Helen eat with a spoon one more time. She helped her scoop up some eggs and brought them to her lips. Helen opened her mouth and took a bite. Annie took Helen's free hand and spelled "good girl."

By noon, Helen had learned to eat with a spoon and fold her napkin. The dining room was nothing short of a disaster area. After hours of fighting, Annie had finally broken through to Helen. Discipline was the key to understanding.

Darren J. Butler

The Little House

CAPTAIN KELLER AND KATE were thrilled that Helen had learned to eat with a spoon and fold her napkin, but they were also concerned with Annie's tactics. After hours of fighting and the noises that came from the locked room, Helen's parents felt that Annie was being too rough on Helen.

After supper, Captain Keller and Kate took a stroll across the grounds. The sun had just begun to set, and a gentle breeze carried the sweet aromas of spring. In the distance, a whippoorwill's song echoed.

Captain Keller led Kate towards the circle of boxwood shrubbery near the little garden house. Accompanied by spring flowers and a concrete bench, the grassy area had provided many hours of enjoyment for their daughter.

I'm afraid this isn't going to work, Captain Keller said after a long silence.

Captain? Kate replied in a surprised voice. *Whatever do you mean?*

Helen Keller: Leader Without Sight or Sound

She's just too rough on the girl. We treat our livestock with more respect, he said.

Kate didn't reply at first. Instead, she mustered up the courage to say what was on her mind. *Captain. Miss Sullivan is right. We've spoiled Helen by giving her everything she wants.*

But...

But nothing, she injected. *It's been easier to let her have her way with things. As long as she has been content and not acting unruly, we...we...*

Kate broke down. Her hands hid the tears streaming down her face. She sat on the concrete bench, and Captain Keller took a seat beside her.

Kate. We did what any parent would do. We tried our best...we saw our daughter in need and we did our best to help her.

Help her? Did you see the look on Miss Sullivan's face when Helen put her hand in her plate? Did you? Kate insisted. *She was disgusted.* Kate rose and tried to gain her composure. *Why aren't we disgusted? Why have we let this go on and on?*

What do you want me to say, Kate? Captain Keller sighed. *Neither one of us have any experience with a child who is deaf and blind. We either had to care for her the best we knew how or send her to one of those asylums.*

Kate's jaw dropped. *Never. Arthur Keller don't you ever suggest that again. I had nightmares for weeks after visiting one of them.*

I'm not suggesting that we ship her off. I'm only saying that…

You don't have the answers! I don't have the answers! But maybe Miss Sullivan does, Kate said.

Not accustomed to being talked to this way, Captain Keller stood and turned away. *At what expense, Kate? As rough as she's being with our girl, Helen might end up with a broken arm or leg!*

She is simply doing what we obviously can't do. She's disciplining her! And we have to let her do it.

I'm glad to hear that, a third voice spoke.

The voice came from outside the tall shrubbery. Annie Sullivan stepped through a sliver of an opening and stood in the shadows of twilight. Her dark glasses still sat on the brim of her nose.

Miss Sullivan, Captain Keller addressed.

Captain Keller, she replied.

We were just discussing Helen, Kate added.

Viney told me. I almost never found you.

I planted this shrubbery to give Helen a safe place to play, Captain Keller began. *We used to find her wandering the grounds. At first, we thought she was lost. But then we realized she was exploring. Loving*

Helen Keller: Leader Without Sight or Sound

nature. She spends hours in here sniffing the flowers, touching the branches, playing in the dirt...

Captain Keller's voice had broken and faded into the sounds of the impending night. His faced turned away from them, Annie imagined him close to tears.

Miss Sullivan, Kate said, interrupting the silence. *Is there hope for Helen?*

Annie was taken aback. *Hope? Certainly there is hope. I realize that you must be troubled by what happened this morning, but I assure you that discipline is the key to unlocking her mind.*

Kate took a deep breath. *All right. What happens next?*

Annie straightened herself. *I need to be completely alone with her. Day and night.*

What? Captain Keller asked.

I need Helen to totally depend on me for everything. Food, water, learning. Once she realizes that she can't run back to you, she will do as I tell her to do.

Captain Keller lit his cigar and let the idea of what Annie was suggesting sink in. *What you tell her to do? How do you expect her to understand?*

Oh, she'll understand. After our battle today, she knows how to eat with a spoon and fold her napkin. It may not seem much to you, but it's an incredible start. I'll keep on teaching her the manual alphabet which will lead her to understanding what words are. From words she will move on to sentences and you will be able to communicate with your daughter.

Captain Keller shook his head, but Kate smiled and nodded.

Where will you take her, Miss Sullivan? Kate asked.

Annie contemplated this for a moment. *I've considered several options. Helen needs to be far away from you.*

What? Oh Miss Sullivan, I'm not sure that I can stand to be far away from her for any period of time, Kate said.

I realize that, Mrs. Keller, Annie assured her. *What if Helen believes she is far away from you, but in reality she is just next door?*

I don't understand, Captain Keller said.

If you take her on an extended carriage ride around the estate, Helen will believe she is hours away from Ivy Green. But, you'll bring her back to this little cottage.

Annie pushed back some of the shrubbery to reveal the porch of the Little House.

The garden house? Kate asked.

Yes. Viney said that Helen never goes in there. She'll never recognize it as long as you keep a distance from her so that she won't smell you. You'll be able to

Helen Keller: Leader Without Sight or Sound

see her each day as long as Helen doesn't know you're there. What do you think?

Captain Keller looked to his wife. The expression on her face told him that she was ready to load Helen up in the carriage and begin the journey.

I don't know, Captain Keller said finally.

Kate walked over to him and took his arm. *Captain. It's worth a try. Please.*

Kate packed Helen's belongings, and Annie packed her own. While the Kellers rode Helen around the grounds, Annie prepared the Little House for Helen's arrival. It was nearly nine o'clock when Annie

Helen's bed in the little house that she and Annie Sullivan shared.

heard the carriage stop near the Little House. From the window, she watched Captain Keller lift a sleepy Helen from the carriage and deposit her on the porch. Holding her hands, they led her inside, but Annie stayed a safe distance away. Helen sat on a rug near the fireplace.

She's barely awake, Kate said.

Yes, well I have a feeling it won't last, Annie replied.

Captain Keller moved to the door, nudging his wife to join him. *Let's go, my dear.*

Kate placed a doll in Helen's arms and kissed her on the forehead. As the Kellers made their way out the door, Captain Keller paused and turned back to Annie.

Take care of her, Miss Sullivan.

I will, Captain Keller.

Once the Kellers were out of sight, Annie closed the door and locked it. She turned down her bed and poked the fire. Helen's eyelids were getting heavier by the moment. Soon, the doll slipped from her grasp. Helen teetered a bit and almost fell backwards, but Annie caught her. Instantly, Helen realized this was not the touch of her mother. Her eyes opened wide. She sniffed wildly. Helen sprang from the floor and lashed out at the air trying to find the door.

When she collided with the doorknob, she tugged

at it to no avail. Annie grabbed her by the wrists, but Helen bit her and escaped to the floor. Moving like a small tornado, Helen knocked over anything in her path. She grabbed hold of a quilt at the end of the bed and spun around with it so fast that she wrapped her little body in it like a cocoon. Stumbling, she fell to the floor and rolled out of it, but even that didn't stop her.

Helen crawled along the floor until she encountered a small toy chest. Reaching inside, she flung out anything she could get her hands on hoping that it would hit the lady who had made her eat with a spoon that morning. Annie dodged a rapid fire of things flying at her. She jumped onto the bed and rolled to the other side to shield herself.

The last object Helen yanked out was a doll. Instead of tossing it, she pulled it close to herself and started to rock. A low moaning sound erupted from her. Exhausted, Helen lay on the floor until her eyelids closed and sleep took her away.

Annie kept her distance until she was sure that Helen was sound asleep. Carefully, she picked her up and placed her in the bed next to her own. Annie tucked her in and brushed a strand of hair from her face.

As she climbed into bed, Annie turned out the light and watched the beams of moonlight fall on

Helen as she peacefully slept.

Tomorrow we begin.

The famous water pump, where Helen's life changed, at Ivy Green.

Darren J. Butler

Water

ANNIE DIPPED HELEN'S FINGERS into a cup of water and placed her hand into the girl's palm. "W...a...t...e...r. Water." Over and over Annie repeated the letters in Helen's hand. Helen's expression remained blank. Only when Annie made her repeat the sequence of letters into her own hand did Helen's face change. Anger and frustration took over. Whatever game this was, Helen didn't like it.

"C...u...p." She rubbed Helen's fingers along the side of the white cup. "F...l...o...o...r." With each noun, Helen repeated the letters. After several words, Annie dipped Helen's fingers into the cup of water again and placed Helen's hand in her palm waiting for her to spell to her. All she needed was for Helen to connect one word with the name of an object and the world would open up to her.

Helen's fingers didn't move. They remained limp as if she didn't have a clue which word went with the cool liquid in the cup.

Helen Keller: Leader Without Sight or Sound

A week passed and the only real accomplishment was tolerance. Annie had made Helen tolerate her. She was able to dress her, feed her, and finger spell. Day and night they spelled with Helen's ability to remember the letters growing more powerful each day. But no matter how precise her finger spelling became, Helen didn't understand that she was spelling the names of all the objects around her.

Ready for a break, Annie led her outside. They left the porch and wandered around the side of the house to an old oak tree. Annie lifted Helen into its branches and climbed onto a large limb with her. The warm March breeze brushed against their cheeks, and Helen's brown hair flittered about. Helen took in a deep whiff of the spring air and relaxed against Annie's shoulder. Annie wanted to caress her tiny face, but the child had shown no affection to her. She wouldn't accept hugs or any kind of motherly touch.

Annie heard the soft chirp of a bird. Not far from where they were sitting, a nest held a small chick and an egg ready to hatch. Carefully, Annie picked up the egg and placed it in Helen's hands. Curious, Helen gently felt the egg as it jostled about in her hand. Suddenly, the egg cracked and a chick fought its way out. Helen gasped and smiled at the small creature stirring in her hands.

Darren J. Butler

Helen petted the chick with one finger. Annie spelled c...h...i...c...k into her palm and Helen repeated the motions. But when Annie asked her to identify the creature, Helen spelled c...u...p. Frustrated, Annie picked up the chick and placed it back in the nest. They climbed down from the tree and walked over to the water pump near the back of the main house.

Annie primed the pump with the long black handle. Water gushed out in a steady stream. She placed Helen's hands under the water to wash them. Taking advantage of the moment, she spelled w...a...t...e...r. Helen formed the letters in her palm, but the blank expression of unknowing filled her face.

Annie pulled her away from the pump and into the shade of a tree. Taking Helen's hand into her own, she started from the beginning. She spelled every word she had taught her young pupil.

What are you spelling to her? Kate asked.

Annie looked up to see Kate near the water pump wearing her gardening apron. Her hair was pulled back in a ponytail and there was a smudge of dirt on her cheek.

Anything and everything, Annie replied.
We are very impressed Miss Annie, Kate added.
With what?

Kate took a step forward but Annie held her hand

up to stop her. If the breeze caught her scent, Helen would know she was close by.

Why are you impressed? Annie asked again.

Look at her, Miss Annie. She's behaving like a normal child. I saw you up there in the branches of that tree.

A chick was born in her hand. I wish you could have seen her face, Mrs. Keller. She wants to learn. She hungers for it.

Kate put her basket of flowers on the ground. *When will she realize? When will she learn?*

Annie looked to Helen who was continuing to spell words with her fingers as if she were having a conversation with herself.

I don't know, Annie said finally. *I wish I could make her understand.*

Give her time, Miss Annie. Please don't give up.

As long as you let me work with her, I'll never give up, Mrs. Keller.

For the next week, Annie continued to spell. Helen spelled back every single letter not knowing they were words. She refused to eat with her hands or wipe her mouth with her sleeve. If Annie didn't give her a spoon and a napkin, Helen refused to eat. The tantrums had ended.

By the end of the second week, the Kellers were

ready to have Helen back in their arms. As Annie was buttoning the back of Helen's dress, Captain Keller appeared in the doorway of the Little House.

Good morning, Miss Sullivan.

Good morning, Captain Keller.

It's been two weeks, he reminded her.

Has it? Annie knew exactly to the day how long it had been.

We agreed on two weeks. Now, my wife and I want her to come home, he said.

Annie sat Helen on the side of the bed and put yarn and crocheting needles in her hands. She tried to avoid eye contact with him, but he sensed her unwillingness to comply.

You mustn't feel like a failure, Miss Sullivan. Look at her. If you had told me a month ago that our Helen would be able to sit still long enough to crochet, I would have laughed in your face.

Life is more than crocheting and doing as your told.

Yes, it is, Miss Sullivan. Perhaps Helen isn't ready to communicate the way you want her to, Captain Keller suggested.

I'm ready for her to communicate. I suppose I can keep on doing what I'm doing, but I want her to know what words are. I want her to be able to read and

Helen Keller: Leader Without Sight or Sound

write...

That's what you want.

It's what she wants too, Captain Keller, Annie replied. *Every ounce of her being tells me that she wants to learn.*

Captain Keller nodded. *We're expecting you both in the main house.*

Annie fought back the anger and frustration. Taking a breath, she replied, *We'll be there for supper.*

Captain Keller locked eyes with Annie. *Supper it is.*

He disappeared from the doorway, and Annie turned back to Helen. She placed her hand on Helen's cheek, but Helen pulled away refusing the affection. Annie knelt on the floor next to Helen.

What do I have to do to get through to you? How do I make you understand that this is a bed or this is yarn or this is a dress? You spell the words perfectly, but you have no idea that they are names for everything around you. Oh Helen. If I could just make your fingers understand one of these words, I know the rest would flow through your mind like a raging river of knowledge.

For the rest of the morning and into the afternoon, Annie spelled to Helen. They started with their daily routine of all the nouns in their cottage. They moved to the porch and then to the garden. Just as the sun started its descent, Annie pulled Helen over to the water pump for a drink. Like she had done countless times before, Annie primed the pump and water flowed from the spout. She gave Helen a drink from a cup and spelled *cup* and *water* into her palm. Helen spelled the words back, but Annie noticed a deeper curiosity on her face.

Annie primed the pump again and water flowed freely. She placed Helen's hand under the water and spelled w...a...t...e...r... to her again. As the water flowed over her fingers, Helen's head tilted back and forth as if she were studying the cool substance running over her hands. All of a sudden, Helen's face brightened. She gasped. Her entire body grew rigid. Something from inside of her was desperately trying to escape. Like a volcano erupting, sound forced its way out of her mouth.

"Wah...wah."

Joy filled Helen's face. The water slowed to a trickle and Helen banged on the spout with her hands begging for more. Annie pumped the handle and water gushed forward.

With her hands in the flowing water, Helen spoke again. "Wah...wah!"

Helen reached out for Annie's hand and spelled

Helen Keller: Leader Without Sight or Sound

w...a...t...e...r... into Annie's palm.

She moved Helen's hand to her own cheek and nodded. "Yes! Oh Helen! Yes!"

Helen dropped to the ground and tapped the dirt with one hand and held the other in the air waiting for Annie to spell into it. Annie spelled g...r...o...u...n...d and Helen spelled it back rapidly. She snatched up a handful of the grass and dirt and rubbed it against her cheeks. Helen leapt to her feet and held her hands up to the heavens, the world now at her fingertips.

Helen moved quickly through all the objects around her, attaching the finger movements to the words that represented them. By the end of the afternoon, Helen had learned twenty-nine words and their meanings. The Kellers were shocked and ecstatic with Helen's revelation. Even they knew that Helen's world would never be the same.

But there was another word that Helen wanted to learn that day.

Before going inside for supper, Helen wrapped her arms around Annie and squeezed her tightly. Tears streamed down her rosy cheeks. Annie tried to hold back the tears, but could not. As she embraced Helen, a flood of memories struck her. She imagined the face of her little brother Jimmie who had died so many years ago. Annie had wondered if she would ever be capable of loving anyone like that again.

Helen pulled away from Annie. She tapped her on the arm with one hand and held out her other hand, waiting for the word. Annie took the small hand into her own and began to spell. "T...e...a...c...h...e...r. Teacher."

"The moment I beheld that eager, pathetic little face, I knew my fate was sealed. Henceforth I should belong to her. There would be no release until death parted us. That little Helen would take the place of my brother Jimmie, the only thing in my life I had deeply loved."

—Annie Sullivan

Helen Keller: Leader Without Sight or Sound

Keller, left, and teacher Annie Sullivan.

Darren J. Butler

Helen Keller, A True Citizen Of The World

BORN IN TUSCUMBIA, ALABAMA, Helen Keller began her life as a normal, healthy girl. When a strange fever robbed her of her sight and hearing, her parents had no idea the impact that their daughter would have on the world. Decades after her death, Helen Keller continues to inspire the world with her courage and determination.

After the "miracle at the pump," Helen and Annie continued her education with the manual alphabet. Helen learned the alphabet manually and in raised print, which enabled her to read and write.

Annie and Helen left Ivy Green and went to Boston so that Helen could attend the Perkins Institute. She excelled in her studies! By the time she was ten years old, Helen said, "Someday I shall go to college."

Helen Keller: Leader Without Sight or Sound

In 1898, Helen entered Cambridge School for Young Ladies and began her preparations for Radcliffe College. Throughout it all, Annie Sullivan never left her side. She spelled books to Helen as well as lectures in her college classes. In the fall of 1900, Helen started to Radcliffe College and received her Bachelor of Arts degree in 1904.

After Helen finished her formal education, she continued to study anything and everything around her. Numerous universities gave her honorary degrees to recognize her scholarly achievements.

The Story of My Life began as a serial in the *Ladies Home Journal* and was published as a book in 1903. Today, this autobiography of Helen's life is available in fifty languages! In addition to her own biography, Helen also wrote *Optimisim*, an essay; *The World I Live In; The Song of the Stone Wall; Helen Keller in Scotland; Out of the Dark; Helen Keller's Journal; Teacher, Anne Sullivan Macy; The Open Door; Midstream - My Later Life; My Religion;* and *Let Us Have Faith*.

Helen received numerous awards during her lifetime including the Gold Medal Award from the National Institute of Social Sciences, America's Award for Inter-American Unity, the National Humanitarian Award from Variety Clubs International, and many others.

Darren J. Butler

In 1954, Helen's birthplace—Ivy Green—was made into a permanent shrine. Dedicated on May 7, 1954, officials from the American Foundation for the Blind and other organizations and agencies were present.

Helen won an Oscar for "Helen Keller: In Her Story," a documentary. The award was for the best feature-length documentary of the year. A few years later, *The Miracle Worker* by William Gibson opened on Broadway with Anne Bancroft as Annie Sullivan and Patty Duke as Helen. The play was a tremendous success and was later made into a movie starring Anne Bancroft and Patty Duke in their roles. Each of them won an Oscar for their portrayal of Annie and Helen.

Helen Keller spent her life promoting the needs of deaf and blind individuals. She appeared before legislatures, lectured, and wrote essays and articles. But above all, Helen Keller made people aware of the needs for disabled individuals through her daily life. She showed the world what a disabled individual can accomplish.

After Annie Sullivan died in 1936, Polly Thomson took over as Helen's companion. When Ms. Thomson died in 1960, Mrs. Winifred Corbally stayed by her side until the end of Helen's life.

Of all the places that Helen Keller lived throughout her life, her favorite home was in Easton, Connecticut in a house she called "Arcan Ridge." On June 1, 1968, a few weeks shy of her 88th birthday, Helen Keller died. Her ashes were placed in the National Cathedral in Washington, DC. She was interred next to her teacher, Annie Sullivan, and her companion, Polly Thomson.

Ivy Green
The Helen Keller Birthplace

The Helen Keller Birthplace is truly a national treasure. Each time I visit the grounds, I walk away inspired. The very existence of Ivy Green would not be possible if it were not for the hard work and dedication of the men and women who labor tirelessly to keep the doors open to the public.

Since the late 1954, the Helen Keller Property Board of Directors has volunteered their time to memorialize the birthplace of Helen Keller. When I took over as the play's director in 1999, some of the original board members were still there. Mike McMackin has served on the board of directors for many years and continues to play a vital role in the ongoing development of Ivy Green's future.

Darren J. Butler

Of all the people I've met along the way, I've never met anyone more dedicated to Helen Keller or Ivy Green as Sue Pilkilton, the executive director. I cannot even imagine the number of hours she spends each week on promoting the birthplace as well as promoting tourism for the State of Alabama.

Also, I would be remiss if I didn't mention Keller Johnson-Thompson, the great grand-niece of Helen Keller. She has also worked tirelessly to educate students and adults about Helen Keller and to continue Helen's efforts to fight for individuals with disabilities.

Helen Keller: Leader Without Sight or Sound
Helen Adams Keller

1880 Helen Keller was born on June 27.

1881 At the age of 19 months, Helen was struck with a high fever and lost her hearing and sight.

1886 Helen met with Dr. Alexander Graham Bell who instructed the Kellers to contact the Perkins Institute.

1887 Annie Sullivan became Helen's teacher. She arrived on March 3.

1888-98 Helen attended the Perkins Institute.

1899 Mark Twain recognized Helen's great spirit and intelligence.

1900 Helen enrolled as a student at Radcliffe College.

1903 *The Story of My Life* by Helen Keller was published.

Darren J. Butler

1904 Helen became the first blind and deaf student to graduate from Radcliffe College.

1915 Helen Keller International was founded.

1924 Helen conducted many tours and lectures in the United States.

1925 Helen challenged the Lions International.

1926 Helen met President Calvin Coolidge.

1927-29 Several books published - *My Religion, Midstream, My Later Life at 49.*

1932 Braille was accepted as the world's standard alphabet for the blind.

1937 Helen developed a close relationship with the Japanese people.

1938 Helen Keller's Journal was published.

1941 Helen attended an opera in New York and experienced the music through vibrations.

Helen Keller: Leader Without Sight or Sound

This bust of Helen Keller is on the grounds of Ivy Green in Tuscumbia.

1943-46 Helen visited military hospitals.

1946-57 Helen visited 35 countries for the improvement of handicapped people.

1954 Ivy Green became a national shrine.

1955 Helen received an Oscar Award for the documentary of her life.

1959 *The Miracle Worker* opens on Broadway with Anne Bancroft and Patty Duke.

1961 Helen met President John F. Kennedy.

1961 *The Miracle Worker* began at Ivy Green.

1962 *The Miracle Worker* film was released. Won two Oscars for Anne Bancroft and Patty Duke and nominated for three Oscars (Best Writing, Best Director and Best Costumes).

1964 Helen suffered a stroke and later retired from public life.

1968 Helen died and was entombed at the National Cathedral in Washington, DC.

Helen Keller: Leader Without Sight or Sound

About The Author

Darren J. Butler is the playwright behind *Runaway Home*, *We The People* and *Among Us*, among many others. His play, *Out of Darkness*, chronicles the young life of Anne Sullivan. It is based on his friend and mentor William Gibson's trilogy concept of Anne Sullivan and Helen Keller's life—*Out of Darkness*, *The Miracle Worker* and *The Monday After the Miracle*. Darren is the author of the *Abbie, Girl Spy* book series for children and young adults. Most recently, he released his new novel for children, *Merlin's Curse*. Darren travels to schools as a Writing Specialist and Author in Residence. Students he has worked with have achieved some of the highest scores in the state on the Alabama Direct Assessment on Writing. He continues to work with schools to integrate writing across the curriculum. Most recently, Darren founded Virtual Village Classroom, an online resource for teachers. Teaching writing, reading and math in a virtual world has been a long-time dream of Darren's. The monthly online publication allows teachers and students to work directly with a working writer.